FONTANA

POCKET LIBRARY OF GREAT ART

Plate I. PORTRAIT OF THE ARTIST'S MOTHER
(MADAME COROT, NEE MARIE-FRANCOISE OBERSON)
c. 1845. *Canvas,* 15¼″ × 12⅛″
National Gallery, Edinburgh

JEAN–BAPTISTE

COROT

(1796 – 1875)

text by

JEAN DIETERLE

COLLINS
Fontana Pocket Library of Great Art

The object of this series is to introduce the great artists of the world to the general reader at a price and in a form suitable to his pocket. The greatest pains have been taken to attain faithful reproduction of the true colour values of the paintings, but no mechanical process exists today which can do justice to the full beauty of the original works of art. The publishers will feel rewarded if readers are persuaded to see the masterpieces themselves in the collections and galleries to which they are directed in the text.

On the cover

VILLENEUVE-LÈS-AVIGNON: VIEW FROM THE GARDEN OF THE HOSPICE

c. 1836. Canvas, 14 ¾ × 11″. The Louvre, Paris

Plate 2. GATEWAY OF THE PARK AT SAINT-CLOUD. *c. 1823-24. Canvas,*
8 ⅝″ × 14 ¾″. Private collection

COROT

Corot was born a poet. This accounts for the special quality of his paintings, for the fact that their brilliant simplicity and irresistible charm stir us deeply. We feel his
poetic sensibility in his landscapes: we sense that he was
held spellbound by the awakening of nature as the morning mists are dispelled by the rising sun, and we enter
into his more contemplative mood when he portrayed
in calmer tones the serene hours of the evening.

The gentle skies of the Ile-de-France and the more

Plate 3. LA PROMENADE DE POUSSIN. *c. 1824-28. Canvas, 12 ½ × 19 ⅝".*
Collection Paul Jamot. The Louvre, Paris

vaporous ones of the Roman countryside alike suited
Corot's meditative temperament, and he always shun-
ned the cruder and more brutal light which strips
nature of its supernatural elements.

The nudes of this incomparable master reflect, like
his landscapes, the fresh candor of his mind, and in
them fleshly sensuality is controlled by wide-eyed in-
nocence. However, for all his angelic gentleness, there
is nothing sugary or effeminate about his art. Simply
by following his natural bent, Corot became a complete
artist: nothing diverted him from the trail that his
genius blazed for his inspiration.

His long life, as Théophile Gautier expressed it with
romantic eloquence, "was cradled on the knees of the
nymphs"—the nymphs who, in obedience to the artist's

Plate 4. GENOA: VIEW FROM THE PASSEGGIATTA DELL'ACQUASOLA.
June 1834. Canvas, 12 ½ × 19 ½". The Art Institute of Chicago

brush, dance endlessly round and round in his honor.

One of the earlier masters of whom Corot reminds us was Claude Lorrain, another very sensitive soul and an ancestor to be proud of. However, Corot was more conscious of his debt to the works of Sebastiano del Piombo.

The prosperous family business in women's apparel did not appeal to the young painter, who already dreamed of another career altogether. But his father held that painting was a lazy man's trade, and apprenticed his son to a draper. Young Corot stayed with him for eight years. Finally, realizing that because of his son's passion for painting and drawing he would never be a good businessman, Monsieur Corot Père spoke to him in a way that indicates great practical good sense: "I was going to give you a hundred thousand

Plate 5. PORTAL OF THE CATHEDRAL OF VÉZELAY.
1841. Canvas, 14 × 18". Private collection

francs to buy yourself a business, but as it is, all you'll get will be two thousand francs a year. That will teach you a lesson. Now, go and have your fun!''

Later Corot would tell amusingly how he had never forgotten his father's parting advice, and that he had indeed enjoyed himself all his life long. So much for the artist's unpromising early years.

He was twenty-six years old when he made friends with the painter Michallon, who influenced him. After Michallon's premature death, Corot painted in the studio of Victor Bertin. The latter, representative of the classical school, equated harmony with symmetry, and his method thus stressed precise draftsmanship above

Plate 6. A VALET. *c. 1845-50. Canvas, 12 ⅞ × 9 ½″. Private collection*

all else. Under his influence Corot "tightened" his drawing, and this by no means hurt the subsequent development of his art. He was often to say in later years: "Draw, draw, you must always draw."

When he set out to make a study from nature, after he had chosen the size of canvas he would use, he made a light sketch in chalk, indicating the values by a more or less transparent scumble. Even before the colors were applied, gentle harmonies appeared on the canvas. Corot was fond of fluid colors and avoided impasto.

Bertin took Corot to Italy and introduced him to the director of the Villa Medici. But Corot, enchanted by the Roman countryside, visited it often and made studies that his colleagues found hard to understand. They were baffled by his artlessness, his beginner's scrupulousness, and his way of faithfully interpreting nature without altering or embellishing it.

Many years later, one of his friends, a famous painter, seeing one of these early works hung in Corot's studio in Paris, said: "We laughed at you a great deal in those days. Well, we were all blind, and it was you who saw clearly."

Of all artists, including the Italians, Corot is the one who best portrayed Italian sites. After three trips to Italy, his love for that country never abated, and even at the end of his life his works are impregnated with recollections of Civita Castellana, the lake of Nemi, Ariccia, and many other spots he cherished, and made famous in his paintings.

A great deal has been written about this master and his work, so we shall confine ourselves to mentioning a few traits to round off his personality.

He was far from uneducated, as has wrongly been asserted; he had studied at the Collège de Rouen. He had a particular preference for Racine and Virgil, and this is understandable considering that these authors

Plate 7. PIERREFONDS (OISE): GENERAL VIEW. *c. 1840-45.*
Canvas, 19 ¼ × 29 ¾″. Museum, Quimper

were endowed with great sensitivity. He was easily in-
spired to enthusiasm, and recited poetry with the same
passion he showed when he spoke about the Pastoral
Symphony or Gluck's arias, for he loved music and
regularly attended the concerts at the Conservatory.

He liked to sing the old French songs, and after
rattling off a great Italian aria, would launch into *Les
Deux Canards*.

He proved his generosity on countless occasions, and
never turned away anyone who needed help. He did
not become famous until late in life, and at the age of
forty he was rejected by the Salon. Fortunately time
avenged him, and subsequently his reputation has kept
steadily growing.

He was well-to-do and, by the standards of his epoch,
even wealthy, but this never changed his calm way of

life—he always, for example, kept the same little studio in the Rue du Faubourg Poissonnière. His apartment was small and unpretentious. One old servant, whose name was Adèle, looked after him and nagged him. His only extravagance was to bring happiness to others. "I give my money away instead of saving it," he would say, "so I have the pleasure of seeing happy people around me while I am alive. No one is interested in my death. Why should I keep my heirs waiting?" He sometimes talked with friends about matters that occupied his mind, such as the divine presence, and once had occasion to express his faith by painting a Calvary for the church at Ville-d'Avray. A great admirer of nature, he communicated his love of it to others.

His mother lived to enjoy his success. He was profoundly attached to her, but judging by what he said about her, she must have been totally unfamiliar with the world in which "Monsieur Camille," as she called him when she was angry with him, lived. He was in his sixties when he related smilingly that one day, at the end of a family dinner, he had lifted his glass with a toast "To Venus and Bacchus." "Monsieur Camille," his mother said angrily, "you have just hurt me very much." She burst into uncontrollable tears, and although he took her home in a cab and begged her to forgive him, she never did.

Some writers have exploited "Papa Corot's" picturesque blue smock and pipe, suggesting that he was a Bohemian. Actually Corot abhorred Bohemianism, and often scoffed at the way painters of the Romantic school rigged themselves up. He dressed carefully, and wore a blue smock only when he worked. Occasionally he would get so much paint on himself that his face would reflect all the colors of the rainbow, but once he took off his working clothes, he always put back on his spotless black frock coat.

Plate 8. MELANCHOLY. *c. 1850. Canvas, 20 × 14¾″*
Carlsberg Glyptothek, Copenhagen

Plate 9. THE BAY OF NAPLES. *c. 1845. Canvas, 15 ⅝ × 23 ⅝".*
Private collection

During a stay at Pied-Selle in the Ardennes, he was asked as he was leaving the library if he wanted a book for bedtime reading. He chose Bossuet's *Funeral Orations*. No doubt, Bossuet's musical prose reminded him of the eloquent harmonies he himself created in color.

A few days before his death, he made this simple statement which may serve as conclusion to an exemplary life, full of great works and good deeds: "I can't complain of my fate—quite the opposite. For seventy-eight years I have enjoyed good health and have loved nature, painting, and work. My family are good people, I have had good friends, and I think I have never hurt anyone. My portion in life has been a fine one, and far from murmuring against fate, I can only be grateful to it."

Plate 10. SAINT-GERMAIN-EN-LAYE: THE TERRACE.
1852. Canvas, 5⅞ × 14½". Private collection

He died peacefully at the age of seventy-nine, leaving behind the memory of a happy man whose moral balance reflected a mind at peace with God and man, and the memory of a painter-poet who lived to see the dream of his youth come true, thus immortalizing his name.

PLATE 11

Painted about 1833

COROT WITH PALETTE

The Uffizi, Florence
Canvas, 12⅞ × 9¾"

This is Corot's second self-portrait. The first, executed before his first trip to Italy, is in the Louvre. He gave it to his parents before he left; they had asked him to do so because a three-year stay abroad in those days seemed a dangerous adventure.

This second self-portrait, painted ten years after the first, foretells the answer Corot was to give in 1835 to the critics Gustave Planche and Jules Janin who had written of him: "An austere talent, very conscientious, but he will never be popular." Janin was mistaken, and Corot said: "No matter what they think, this is first-rate!" ("First-rate"—*fameux* —was Corot's favorite word.)

Such was the assurance, the masterly authority, tempered as it was by gentleness, that the artist possessed all his life.

This beautiful portrait showing the artist in early manhood hung for a long time in his studio. The left side of the face is in shadow; the chin is slightly protruding; the linen blouse has white highlights; one hand holds the palette, the other the brush.

In 1872 Corot received a letter from the administration of the Uffizi in Florence, asking him for a self-portrait. He did not reply immediately: he had not painted himself since 1835, and he hesitated to send an old portrait. Finally, a few days before his death, early in 1875, he made up his mind to send the one shown here.

PLATE 12

Painted 1833

MADAME CHAMOUILLET NÉE OCTAVIE SENNEGON, COROT'S NIECE

Private collection
Canvas, 13¾ × 11½"

Youth, candor, attentiveness, and simplicity are combined in this delicate portrait. Corot painted it in the home of Monsieur Chamouillet, when he began, between 1830 and 1835, to do the portraits of his close relatives.

If we compare this portrait with any of the ones Corot had painted ten years earlier, before his first trip to Italy, we see the extent to which he had developed. The earlier works suggest a certain timidity, deliberate concentration on a specific goal; here we are dealing with a painter fully conscious of his artistic self.

This calm young face, trying to put on a serious expression, has gentleness, naïveté, and peaceful contentment. The watch on the round table on which she leans her right arm may have been placed there to indicate the time of posing. The hair-do is impeccable, the carnation in the belt repeats the color of the ribbon at the collar.

Was she engaged at the time this was painted? Probably, for she eventually became Madame Léon Chamouillet. Later Corot gave this portrait to his sister, who bequeathed it to her son-in-law; the latter died at the age of ninety-six.

Plate 13. CASTEL SANT'ANGELO AND BRIDGE, WITH CUPOLA OF ST. PETER'S, ROME

VENTE
COROT

(Commentary follows colorplate section)

Plate 14. NARNI: THE BRIDGE OF AUGUSTUS ON THE NERA

PLATE 15

Painted about 1838

SEATED YOUNG WOMAN HOLDING FLOWERS

Museum, Vienna
Canvas, 21½ × 15⅝″

Her name was Madame Legois, and she seems to have been an uncomplicated woman with dreamy eyes. Was she a relative, a milliner, or what? No one knows, but what Corot tried to express in this figure was its aliveness, with all the necessary nuances of transition.

He always worked from the model with patient concentration as well as enjoyment. The delicacy of this attentive face, the extremely refined coloring of the dress, the few flowers in her lap, and the hands as softly modeled as a caress, combine to make an exquisite picture.

The costume may have been put on just for the occasion. It sets off this woman's features, permeated with a gentle sadness and an almost morbid gravity.

The spots of color in the red dress, the ribbon of the same hue in the hair, add animation, if not gaiety, to this perfect ensemble.

It may be noted that Corot, an inveterate bachelor, often portrays women as ideal creatures beyond all thought of attainment. His feminine figures are sometimes true to life, however, so much so that they are apt to disappoint us rather than charm us; sometimes they are gay, and sometimes they have severe or aloof faces. The faces of many of the younger ones express a gentle sadness. They bring to mind what Eugène Fromentin wrote about the figures portrayed by Memling: "They have an indefinable gravity, they seem to have gone through life suffering and thinking about it."

Plate 16. VOLTERRA: VIEW OF THE TOWN

(Commentary follows colorplate section)

PLATE 17

Painted 1835

AVIGNON: VIEW FROM VILLENEUVE

Tate Gallery, London
Canvas, 13¼ × 28¾″

Corot kept this landscape all his life. Like most of his studies from nature, it was executed during the summer, this time on the trip to Provence with Gaspart Lacroix and the orientalist Marilhat, who had come back to France to rest from his strenuous travels in Egypt.

We learn from Corot's letters that at Villeneuve-lès-Avignon there were plenty of wonderful things to do, and that the friends got up at four in the morning and worked until they were famished, and then returned for their midday meal. "We slept until two and then went out again and stayed until dark. To tell the truth, you could smell the garlic on us two miles away, but, then, what salads we had!"

The studious young men salted these memorable salads with gaiety and songs. Corot's voice would ring out to stir up slumbering echoes in the old town, and windows would open when he launched into some old refrain.

On the banks of the Rhône the artist discovered subjects as good as those he had painted in Italy. The view shown here brings to mind his early landscapes, such as *La Promenade de Poussin* (plate 3). It continues the inspiration which called forth his highest gifts. The sensitive line achieves perfection in the way the contour of the hills harmonizes so beautifully with the sky.

In his notebooks Corot wrote: "Draw the motif in its purity, after you have set down the effect you want on gray paper; then paint the picture part by part, as fully as possible at the first try, so that only

a very little is left to be done after everything has been covered with paint. I have noticed that something done at the first try is more direct, more attractive, and that it is often possible to take advantage of accidents; whereas if one does a thing over, one often loses the original color harmony."

The color harmony of this landscape is truly musical.

PLATE 18

Painted 1844

OCTAVE CHAMOUILLET PUSHING A WHEELBARROW IN THE GARDEN

Collection R. Delapalme, Paris
Canvas, 6 ⅛ × 7 ¾″

This painting is not mentioned in *L'Oeuvre de Corot* by Moreau Nélaton and Alfred Robaut. It belonged to the painter Maurice Lard, and later, to his daughter, and has only recently been discovered.

Corot had come upon his nephew in a corner of the garden. The child's surprise is shown in this work. The young gardener, in striped trousers, with a large apron to protect his white shirt, his sleeves carefully rolled up, his delicate face shaded by a large straw hat, stopped short when he caught sight of his uncle at a turn in the path.

Corot was fond of movement, and we feel that the child is not going to stay still much longer—that he will go on to empty the wheelbarrow he has not had the time to set down.

Corot's models were allowed to move around—he never minded this. Those who knew him took advantage of it, and his favorite model, the little Dobigny, used to chatter and sing, and never kept still for a moment. One day a friend took exception to her casual behavior. "But it's precisely the restlessness that I like," Corot said. "I'm not a specialist doing a job, my aim is to express life. I have to have a model who moves about."

Corot never learned the sad fate of this nephew of his. Octave died at the age of twenty-six in Buenos Aires, far away from home.

PLATE 19

Painted about 1845

PORTRAIT OF EDOUARD LESCOT
AT VILLE-D'AVRAY

Private collection
Canvas, 10¾ × 8½"

This masterpiece, like sixteenth-century portraits, did not have to be big.

When he got back from his trips to Italy or into the French countryside, Corot often painted the likenesses of people he was fond of, such as his friend Lescot's boy. He had also painted portraits of his sister, his mother, and all his nephews and nieces. We may recall that at this time photography had not begun to rival painting.

It is extraordinary how well Corot, who had no children, expressed in this painting the awakening mind of the child, his eager desire to participate in life, his attentive wonder at the world he is discovering.

This portrait, which Alfred Robaut did not know, was painted at Ville-d'Avray, in an eighteenth-century house Corot's parents purchased in 1817—a house that Corot never gave up.

"This house witnessed some interesting events that took place long ago. On the night of July 27, 1794, Monsieur de Talleyrand, Bishop of Autun, took refuge there on the night of Thermidor."

PLATE 20

Painted 1851

LA ROCHELLE:
ENTRANCE TO THE PORT

Private collection
Canvas, 10¼ × 14¾"

This is one of the best of the studies Corot executed at La Rochelle.

The port with its sails and mastheads, and the old towers looming in the blue summer sky were painted under the friendly and ironical eyes of Corot's fellow painters, Comeiras and Brizard. They were amazed at the conscientiousness which was always holding up the progress of his work, and every day teased him with the same question: "Don't tell us you're going to start that sketch all over again today?"

Corot spent ten or twelve days painting this view. He lodged with a wholesale merchant, an art lover, Monsieur Moulun, who kept a number of Corot's studies on the walls of his house in the Rue Porte-Neuve.

Corot succeeded here in holding fast to his idea of what the "motif" of the scene should be, and thus endowed it with more than usual subtlety and life. The docks and towers are bathed in light. One has to see this smooth light at the end of a September afternoon, when it seems like shimmering mother-of-pearl. This is the sky that Fromentin described in his novel *Dominique*.

PLATE 21

Painted about 1845

THE BRIDE

The Louvre, Paris
Canvas, 12½ × 9⅜″

This was the painter Cibot's maid. One day Corot
met Cibot who told him that his maid was about to
get married, and that he had promised to paint her
in her wedding gown. "Would you like to share the
model with me?" he asked. Corot accepted the
offer at once.

When he told this incident to Robaut, pointing
to the portrait hanging on his studio wall, Corot
said: "She is first-rate, one of the best in the store."
The term "store" stood for the canvases he kept in
his studio, just as in Madame Corot's store it de-
noted dresses. Remembering this conversation, Alfred Robaut bought this portrait at the sale of
Corot's works held after his death.

Corot treated his subject with the painstaking
candor of the Flemish portraitists. The oval of the
face, of unusual purity, further emphasized by the
black hair parted in the middle, is seen under a
transparent veil. The gleaming whites on the satin
dress bring to mind the famous lesson of the *Bouquet*
that Largillierre gave to Oudry.

Plate 22. ROSNY (SEINE-ET-OISE): CHÂTEAU OF THE DUCHESS DE BERRY

COROT. 18

(*Commentary follows colorplate section*)

PLATE 23

Painted about 1855–58

NYMPH RECLINING ON THE GRASS

Museum, Geneva
Canvas, 18⅜ × 24½"

Brilliant and luminous, this nymph is a woman, and nothing lets one forget that fact. The very breath of nature moves across the composition. The harmony is remarkable; the nude body is supple and its pose quiet and relaxed.

Did this nymph remind the artist of an old love? Did he smile as he painted her, recalling the letters he sent to his friend Osmond during his first trip to Italy? "Don't ever go through Bologna, the city is too full of enchanting sirens. I let myself be seduced by the prettiest ballerina of the Bologna opera house, and I have kept a very pleasant recollection of her. Roman women are the most beautiful I know. Their eyes, shoulders, hands are superb."

And yet his purchasers grumbled not only against his figures, but also against his nudes. The concensus was that Corot was a landscapist who was not good at portraits, which he would have done better to leave to "specialized portrait painters."

The seeming awkwardness of Corot's figures baffled most of his fellow painters. Ingres, who one day ran into him in the studio of Haro (an expert portraitist), on seeing one of his Venuses, left precipitously to avoid saying what he thought of it. Hippolyte Flandrin, more perceptive and less partisan, asserted that Corot put into his figures something that the specialists never put in theirs.

PLATE 24

Painted about 1865–70

MANTES: THE CATHEDRAL AND THE CITY SEEN THROUGH TREES

Museum, Rheims
Canvas, 20 × 12½"

At this lovely hour, the poet finds only a single fisherman about, while in the water all the shades of daylight are breaking up. Water was one of Corot's great passions, for it gratified his subtle taste for changing tones, a perpetual threat to form. But how well he rendered the character of these misty hours: one silvery willow in the gray dawn enlivens with its delicacy a background only slightly more compact.

Through the branches we see the cathedral in the middle of the city, hovering over the houses as if to protect them.

Corot often took cathedrals for subjects, after he left Paris in 1830 to avoid the revolutionary disturbances. Prompted by his friend Poirot, an artist who specialized in medieval architecture, he began by painting the magnificent structure at Chartres. Corot was not an architect, but he had a good knowledge of architecture and perspective, and he would have been shocked by the ignorance of modern artists who take no trouble to learn even the rudiments of this difficult art.

Chartres, Vézelay, Sens, Mantes—these glories of France—were all admirably portrayed by Corot. The beautiful drawing, the arrangement, the gentle atmosphere, the sky which is at one with the building, epitomize his art, his subtlety, his special style.

Plate 25. MANTES: FERRYMAN WITH VIEW OF THE BRIDGE

(Commentary follows colorplate section)

PLATE 26

Painted about 1840–45

LAKE OF GENEVA: THE QUAI DES PAQUIS

Museum, Geneva
Canvas, 14 × 18"

After he had stopped a while in the Dauphiné, Corot went on to spend the rest of the summer in Switzerland. There he stayed with friends, a Monsieur Giraud and his son-in-law Armand Leleux, a pupil of Ingres who lived at Dardagny near Geneva.

Both Leleux and his wife were artists. In their home Corot met several local painters, not to mention fellow Parisians, such as Baron and Daubigny.

Corot's dark blue smock caused an amusing misunderstanding. The village priest one day saw Corot painting next to Leleux out in the country and said to the latter: "Well, well, Monsieur Armand, I see outdoor painting is doing fine these days, isn't it?" And noting Leleux's surprise, he added: "Surely your trade is doing well if you brought a worker along to help you!" Leleux tried to explain to the priest that the great artist was modestly concealing himself in his working clothes, and spoke eloquently of Corot's talent, and of the generous help he always gave the poor. Then the priest exclaimed, "I see, this is the Saint Vincent de Paul of painting!" This felicitous phrase caught on.

Corot stayed in Switzerland several weeks, and executed this masterpiece there, pure, luminous, and great in its simplicity.

PLATE 27

Painted about 1868–70

GREEK GIRL

Collection Mrs. J. Watson Webb, New York
Canvas, 32 5/8 × 13 1/4"

Degas one day (June 20, 1887) said to Frémiet: "In my opinion Corot can draw a tree better than any of us, but I think his figures, too, are superior."

At the time this great artist's judgment was apt to surprise art lovers who did not know about this masterpiece or paid no attention to it. It represents one of Corot's favorite models, Emma Dobigny, and dates from a time not long before his death. Jules Dupré said of him that he painted, "with wings on back," certain Jewish models who at the time were to be found at the Bal de l'Astic in the Rue Saint-Antoine. Their figures decorated the walls of his studio. He passed on their addresses to Eugène Delacroix, along with his appreciations, saying of Madame Hirch, for instance, "A superb head, along the lines of Ristori," and "Adèle Rosenfeld in a reclining pose seemed to me superb."

Garbed in studio costumes, as was customary in the period, these girls were painted as Eurydice, Judith, as characters in Italian novels, or as heroines of Greek mythology.

Anticipating Manet, these figures are already painted as though out-of-doors. It was by his technical innovations that Corot influenced his generation so strongly.

Plate 28. MEMORY OF THE COUNTRYSIDE AROUND SAINT-OMER

(Commentary follows colorplate section)

PLATE 29

Painted 1871

THE BELFRY OF DOUAI

The Louvre, Paris
Canvas, 18 × 14¾"

This view was painted from a window in the second floor of a house at the corner of the old Rue du Pont-à-l'Herbe and the Rue de la Cloies. It took Corot nearly twenty sittings of four hours each (from 2 to 6 in the evening) to execute it. On May 8 he wrote to Desavary who was then at Arras: "I am putting the finishing touches on the Belfry of Douai, a splendid work."

He was right, it is a splendid work, one of his finest. The aged artist, now close to his death, here resumed his grand style: this painting is equal to the Port of La Rochelle (plate 20), and the "views" of Avignon. The gray houses are well set; the ageless light plays over the ancient stone; the spots formed by the old shops, the gentle provincial atmosphere, the roof tops, and even the geranium on a window sill of the tower—are these not one great poem to light? The subtle atmosphere, the flawless drawing, the sky perfectly harmonized with the building, does not all this epitomize Corot?

"Infallible rigor of harmonies and profound sense of construction," Baudelaire wrote of him in 1859, and Maxime du Camp, in the *Revue des Deux-Mondes*, praised him as follows: "Monsieur Corot possesses a remarkable quality that most contemporary artists lack. He can create.... His point of departure is always nature, but when he comes to the point of interpretation, he stops copying, he remembers, and at once achieves a superior, altogether sublimated approach."

PLATE 30

Painted 1874

WOMAN IN BLUE

The Louvre, Paris
Canvas, 31 ⅛ × 19 ½"

On October 29, 1874, a Committee was formed to present the great artist with the tribute that had been denied him by the sectarianism of the cliques. For, though he had been elected member of the Commission des Artistes by a large majority, he had not been awarded the Medal of Honor.

A medal engraved by Geoffroy Dechaume was presented to him at a gathering at the Grand Hôtel. Corot, surrounded by all his friends, was deeply moved. It was a simple ceremony, without speeches; Corot's illness, which had almost kept him from attending, cast its shadow over the gathering.

Corot left very early and went back home in pain. He could not doubt now that this was his last illness; and yet, in this year of 1874, with death lying in wait for him, at the peak of his talent, he painted one important work: a full-length figure which, at this early date, anticipates Renoir.

Corot was indeed a precursor. Degas, who was an expert, and was not given to compliments, said to Pissarro at the Paton Auction in 1883: "Corot is still the biggest one of all, he saw everything that was coming."

This pensive woman, who is resting her elbows on a credenza, her dress falling in folds of marvelous color, would be enough alone to make an artist famous.

This is French art at its most delightful best in the period of the Second Empire which ended in 1875. Corot, Baudry, Renoir, and in sculpture Carpeaux, all expressed the feminine charm of that epoch.

Painted about 1826

CASTEL SANT'ANGELO AND BRIDGE, WITH CUPOLA OF ST. PETER'S, ROME

Private collection
Canvas, 15⅝ × 20¾″

The famous setting that provided the motif of this work so struck Corot during his first trip to Italy that he did it several times. This is the best of the various studies, and is mentioned by Alfred Robaut in his book, though he had not seen it. It is remarkable for the firmness of the drawing in the gentle golden light, a light that is characteristic of Corot's early works, which come close to a direct vision of nature.

When Corot painted his favorite subjects in 1825 he produced masterpieces. He did not have to find himself: all he needed was the Italian skies. Throughout his long career he painted many magnificent works, always expressing the nobility of nature, but none were more beautiful than this one.

Only three years earlier he had been a draper's apprentice, busy measuring out fabrics by the yard. No memories of famous precursors intervened between him and nature. He possessed an instinctive lucidity. He did without formulas, without theories. Like a primitive, he chose a beautiful motif, fixed its setting, and tried to be as exact as possible. He reproduced stones, vegetation, light, and faint shadows.

His vision of nature is bathed in some tender spell, and the images vouchsafed him are transformed into rich and faithful paintings.

Painted 1826

NARNI: THE BRIDGE
OF AUGUSTUS ON THE NERA

The Louvre, Paris
Paper on canvas, 14 × 18⅜″

Really to grasp Corot's greatness, one must go to the Louvre and examine this study, one of his most beautiful. Of all his various manners, this is one of the most enchanting.

The painting shows a large blue plain, at the end of a valley. Another painter would probably have forced it into perspective, creating a hole. But here the lovely pigment ties together all the parts of the horizon. There is no break in the harmony; here the eye moves from the nearest to the farthest plane by the gentlest transitions. Corot scarcely ever attained greater richness of texture, subtle and at the same time solid.

The artist was thrilled by the view, and he utilized this study for a large composition he sent to the Salon of 1827.

Very unlike contemporary artists, painters at that period, after working up a motif from nature to their liking, used these sketches in the winter, when they set out to compose their large historical paintings for the Salon, the only exhibition held every other year.

In this painting Corot anticipated Cézanne, who was, as a matter of fact, deeply impressed by it, studied it thoroughly, and often turned back to it.

Painted June, 1834

VOLTERRA: VIEW OF THE TOWN

The Louvre, Paris
Canvas, 27⅜ × 36⅝″

This is probably the painting that was exhibited at the Salon of 1849 as No. 439.

Corot, who could catch the line of a hill with a single stroke of pen or brush, captured the significant contours of this admirable landscape with great assurance. "Never leave anything uncertain in whatever you do," he used to say. He lovingly recorded every detail of olive trees, pines, underbrush, rocks. Then he began to paint, giving full sway to his genius. He set down the colors in their exact values, and here they have the quality of fresh fruit. There is "first-rate work" underneath all this.

Copying his motifs with a youthful sincerity that amused his fellow students at the Villa Medici, he painted such sites as he saw them. At the same time, he instinctively chose places perfectly suited to what he wanted to express. Nowhere are Corot's qualities so evident as here.

This work, which marks the debut of a great master, shows him in full possession of his means. In one of his notebooks he referred to Volterra as "magnificent countryside." He arrived there on June 22, 1834, and his admiration was translated into a series of important works, to which he devoted long hours on fine hot days. He left this enchanting place for Florence, where he arrived on July 21.

Painted 1840

ROSNY (SEINE-ET-OISE):
CHÂTEAU OF THE DUCHESS DE BERRY

The Louvre, Paris
Canvas, 9 × 12⅞"

This painting, which was a gift from Corot to his friend Madame Osmond, shows the château as it had looked before two of the wings were demolished. Near the center we see a lady painting, and two children watching her. She may have been Madame Osmond, a relative of Corot's who lived in an old priory adjacent to the church of Rosny with her husband, Abel Osmond. It was he who brought Corot here, and he was fascinated by this part of the country, not far from Mantes. His hostess was kind and considerate, and arranged a studio for Corot in a small building where he could paint in peace. To work like this among friends was what he liked best.

Every year in July the landscapist, his bag slung over his shoulders, explored the countryside at day-break. Occasionally he found his motif right outside the house. He might paint a view of the church seen from the orchard, or, on another occasion, paint this old château with its slate roof and its brick façade, with its blues and reds mingled with the green of the trees.

One Sunday as she was leaving mass, Madame Osmond said to Corot: "Camille, it would be so lovely of you if you painted something for our church." Corot painted *The Flight into Egypt* (exhibited at the Salon of 1840) using the landscape of the Seine at Bonnières. The Virgin was Mademoiselle Varin, daughter of the local stone cutter.

Does not this study of the château at Rosny contain in itself the whole of Impressionism?

Painted about 1868–70

MANTES: FERRYMAN WITH VIEW
OF THE BRIDGE

The Louvre, Paris
Canvas, 14¾ × 21⅞″

This river scene, with the red-capped fisherman, the vigorous trees rising in the foreground, the roofs seen through the alders, and the old bridge at Mantes, which Corot painted many times, shows him at the height of his genius. There is a close relation between his art and orchestral music, which, incidentally, Corot worshiped.

His paintings were successful because no other painter in any period has displayed gentleness and firmness to such almost equal degrees, such feeling for nature, such depth of emotion, and such expertness at rendering this hour of dawn which Victor Hugo, too, evoked in an immortal line: *La nature tranquille et superbe renaît* ("Tranquil and superb, nature is being reborn…").

The man who made this was all painter—all French painter. Italy and the fashionable chatter of the studios during his youth had revealed to him the beauty of simple outlines, but he had a special love for France where just such bluish outlines are to be found along with these bluish mists, these broken tones in her skies, these delicate greens. Never before had he painted more joyful grays, more silvery tones; here he is resolutely, grandiosely lyrical, and if we have followed the artist's works from 1822 to 1870, we are deeply stirred. There is calm grandeur in this work, its composition is flawless and strictly harmonious.

Corot used to say that a landscape painter must "at least have the patience to let the mists rise and slowly penetrate his landscape, and, once he is in it, to enjoy it."

Painted 1869

MEMORY OF THE COUNTRYSIDE AROUND SAINT-OMER

Private collection
Canvas, 22¾ × 31½"

Was not Corot a prophet in what he wrote, about 1852, after he had been asked to paint some landscapes which were to be as far removed from nature as possible? Quite unable to paint a landscape that did not exist, he replied: "I cannot succeed in imagining trees other than the way they grow in nature.... Now, I'm wondering, the way things are going, is this the future? We shall see." A case of foreknowledge, perhaps.

In this surprising little-known painting Corot displayed unusual boldness in using the powerful tree with branches defying the sky to give firmness to his motif. We are reminded of La Fontaine's fable about the oak tree and the reed, but there is no storm in the air, the countryside is calm, and the extraordinary light of the north that only Corot rendered so well is reflected in the pond. A curious cow has turned her head toward the painter, astonished by his open umbrella, and probably sorry that she has stirred from her torpor. Farms in the distance serve as balance between the right and the left sides of the motif.

Corot's conception of the forms of the terrain and the trees is both circular and wavy. These amazing clumps of trees that soar like compact round flames are nevertheless tied to the soil with gentle vigor.

Saint-Omer is a flat country, bathed in luminous mists of brilliant colors whose shimmer gives the coats of the domestic animals a jewel-like tone and transforms the entire landscape into one great painting full of colorful crystallizations around brilliant spots of color.

Plate 31. VIEW OF A PORT IN BRITTANY. *c. 1850-60. Canvas,*
15 ⅝ × 21 ¾". Collection Oscar Reinhart, Winterthur

BIOGRAPHICAL NOTES

1796   Jean-Baptiste Camille Corot is born in Paris on July 16.

1807   Enters Collège de Rouen.

1812-14 Boards at Poissy, where he completes his studies.

1822-25 Obtains from his parents permission to devote himself to painting. Takes a few lessons from Michallon, then studies under Jean Bertin for three years. First sketches after nature.

1825-28 Studies at Fontainebleau. First trip to Italy. Paints in Rome, Terni, and Montecavo. Visits La Sabina, Civita Castellana, Ronciglione, Sant'Elia. In November 1826 makes studies at Albano, Ariccia, Marino, and Frascati, and in the spring of 1828 at Naples, Ischia, and Venice.

Plate 32. YPORT: BEACH, VIEW TOWARD FÉCAMP. *1872.*
Canvas, 9¾ × 27¾". Private collection

1830-31 Paints the Paris quais with his friend Poirot.
Leaves Paris with him during the revolution to
paint architectural studies at Chartres (the cathedral). Then goes to Normandy, to Burgun-
dy, to Auvergne, to Morvan, but he does not
forget Fontainebleau (the forest).

1833   Awarded a second prize at the Salon. Stays at
Rouen with Sennegon. In May visits Monsieur
Henry at Soissons.

1834   Second trip to Italy. Spends twenty days at
Genoa, then goes to Tuscany (view of Volterra). In August he goes to Venice, then visits
the lake region, Desenzano, Riva, Como, and
travels back to France via Switzerland.

1839-40 The Duc d'Orléans buys two paintings from
him. Théophile Gautier publishes a poetic eulogy
of his painting *Evening* at the Salon; the critics
begin to be kinder. The government buys his
Little Shepherd at the Salon.

Plate 33. GIRL READING. c. 1855-60. Canvas, 25 ³/₈ × 27 ³/₄″.
Collection Oscar Reinhart, Winterthur

Plate 34. ITALIAN GIRL PLAYING THE MANDOLIN IN THE STUDIO.
c. 1865-70. Canvas, 23 3/8 × 18 3/4". Collection Oscar Reinhart, Winterthur

Plate 35. WOMAN WITH A PEARL. *c. 1868-70.*
Canvas, 27 ¾ × 21 ⅛". The Louvre, Paris

Plate 36. DIANA AND HER COMPANIONS. *1855.*
Canvas, 7′6″ × 8′6″. Museum, Bordeaux

1843   Third trip to Italy. Visits Tivoli, Genzano, the lake of Nemi, and then Rome.

1847   Meets Eugène Delacroix.

1849   Member of the jury, he begins to be recognized as one of the leading artists of the contemporary school.

1855   Universal Exposition. Awarded Medal First Class. Napoleon III buys *Recollection of Marcoussis.*

1862   Visit to England with his friend Jules Badin; paints three studies there.

1866-67 The Emperor buys his painting *Solitude* for 18,000 francs. Nominated *officier* of the Légion d'Honneur. Must travel less because of illness.

1870   During the war, sells paintings and gives the proceeds to help the poor.

1871   During the Commune stays at Arras, where he executes the magnificent *Belfry of Douai.*

Plate 37. INTERIOR OF SENS CATHEDRAL. *September 1874.*
Canvas, 23 ³⁄₈ × 15 ⁵⁄₈". The Louvre, Paris

Plate 38. PASTURE NEAR SAINT-LÔ. *Pen drawing.*
11 × 17 ½". Former Collection Dubuisson

1872   Visits his oldest friend, Jules Badin, at the Man-
        ufacture de Beauvais, and then goes to Fumay
        and Pied-Selle. In July, visits Jules Dieterle at
        Criquebœuf near Yport. In November, he un-
        dertakes to support a children's home. He buys
        the house occupied by Daumier and gives it to
        him as a birthday present. Paints *Le Départ pour
        la promenade*.

1874   Is refused the Medal of Honor. Despite his ad-
        vancing illness, his eye preserves all its keenness,
        and he paints the remarkable *Interior of Sens
        Cathedral*. Deeply affected by the death of his
        sister, Madame Sennegon. Attends a gathering
        at which his friends and admirers present him
        with a medal, "In admiration of his work,
        1822-1874."

1875   Learns of the death of Jean-François Millet and
        sends money to his widow. On February 22,
        dies of cancer of the stomach.

Plate 39. ROME: OUTSIDE THE VILLA MEDICI.
1827. Pen and sepia. The Louvre, Paris

Plate 40. HIDE-AND-SEEK. *1858.* "*Glass etching,*" *9 × 6 ½"*

BIBLIOGRAPHY

RIENAEKER, V., ed. *Paintings and Drawings of J. B. C. Corot in the Artist's Own Collection.* Minton, 1929.

SERULLAZ, M. *Corot.* Zwemmer, 1951.

The definitive work is:

ROBAUT, A. *L'oevre de Corot: Catalogue raisonné et illustré.* 4 vols. Floury, Paris, 1905. *Suppléments I and II par A. Schoeller et J. Dieterle.* Paris, 1948 and 1956.

NOTE ON THE "GLASS ETCHINGS"

In 1853, Corot's friends at Arras, passionately interested in the new medium of photography, had the idea of drawing a sketch with a needle on a plate of glass covered with collodium. They thus obtained a negative. These "inventors" baptized this technique "glass etchings." In 1903 Hédiard, without too much enthusiasm, called it *"procédé sur verre"* ("glass process").

Corot became interested in this technique and obtained striking effects with it. He engraved about forty plates; like all geniuses he was an engraver even before making any engravings. His incisive stroke recalls Rembrandt. His finest "glass etchings" are *Le Cavalier en Forêt, Le Bois de l'Ermite, Le Souvenir d'Ostie*—blond proofs on paper, of an incomparable transparency, where the bluish stroke is varied with old gold reflections.

PRINTED 1960 IN ITALY

OFFICINE GRAFICHE GARZANTI - MILANO